A

Literature Unit

for

The Cat in the Hat

by Dr. Seuss

Written by Susan Williams

Teacher Created Materials, Inc.
P.O. Box 1040
Huntington Beach, CA 92647
©1995 Teacher Created Materials, Inc.
Made in U.S.A.

ISBN 1-55734-540-6

Illustrated by Barb Lorseyedi

Edited by Barbara Levy

Cover Art by Ron Zeilinger

Table of Contents

Introduction and Sample Lessons

Children of all ages have become friends with Dr. Seuss through his wonderful use of rhyme, repetition, and colorful characters. Dr. Seuss makes beginning reading fun, and children can find success as they memorize their favorite rhymes. They then begin the decoding process which occurs naturally with repeated readings. When young readers are introduced to the language of Dr. Seuss, they will want to hear and read his books over and over again. Teachers will find that this literature unit will help them guide their students through *The Cat in the Hat* with a variety of activities that focus on beginning reading skills, including rhyming, listening, speaking, writing, vocabulary, comprehension, and word recognition skills.

A Sample Lesson Plan

A detailed sample lesson plan is provided on page 4. Each lesson can be completed in one day or may be extended to suit the needs of the class. Refer to the Suggestions for Using the Unit Activities on pages 7–10 for information and ideas relating to each activity.

A Unit Planner

A blank unit planner is provided on page 5 for you to write your own lesson plans. Reproduce copies of the Unit Planner as needed.

Sample Lesson Plan

Lesson 1

- Introduce the book by using some or all of the Setting the Stage unit activities. (page 7)
- Read Getting to Know the Book and the Author to students. (page 6)
- Read the story orally to the students.
- Play one or more of the Rhyme Card Games. (page 14)
- Homework: Assign House Rules. (page 40)

Lesson 2

- Discuss and chart results of House Rules homework.
- Have students reread orally with you.
- Discuss Story Questions. (page 18)
- Play Rhyme Card Games. (page 14)
- Complete with partners or independently Rhyme Detective. (pages 22 and 23)
- Homework: Assign Weather Makes A Difference. (page 37)

Lesson 3

- Reread story orally in groups.
- In same groups, create books using Sentence Strips. (pages 16 and 17)
- Do Tricks. (page 44)
- Homework: Assign Hats. (page 39)

Lesson 4

- Students orally read their created books (from previous day) to class.
- Complete "Who Said That?" (page 20) and A Portrait of the Cat in the Hat. (page 21)
- Practice Sequence Sentence Strips in pocket chart. (pages 16 and 17)
- Homework: Assign Picture Dictionary (page 24) and The Scrambler. (page 26)

Lesson 5

- Create stick puppets (page 25) and do dramatizations.
- Complete Calling All Adjectives. (page 32)
- Complete Math Code. (page 35)
- Homework: Assign Crossword Puzzle. (page 29)

Lesson 6

- Practice and tape record the Recorded Story. (page 28)
- Create House Frame Poem. (page 19)
- Homework: Assign Other Cats in Hats. (page 42)

Lesson 7

- Have students read orally with partners their favorite part.
- Complete Context Clues. (page 30)
- Make Seuss-Arama Triaramas. (page 27)
- Homework: Assign Cat Report. (pages 45 and 46)

Lesson 8

- Listen to Recorded Story (created in Lesson 6) and read along silently.
- Create Painting Seuss-Style and sentence captions. (page 41)
- Homework: Continue Cat Report.
- Assign Reading Wheel (page 33) and Book Review (page 34).

Unit Planner

Unit Activities

Date:

Notes/Comments:

Unit Activities

Date:

Notes/Comments:

Unit Activities

Date:

Notes/Comments:

Unit Activities

Date:

Notes/Comments:

Unit Activities

Date:

Notes/Comments:

Unit Activities

Date:

Notes/Comments:

Getting to Know...

...the Book

(The Cat in the Hat is published in the U.S., Canada, and Australia by Random House. It is also available in the U.K. from Random Century House.)

It is a rainy day, and Sally and her brother can find nothing to do. Suddenly, in comes the Cat and that's when the trouble begins! The pet fish reminds the children that the Cat should not be in the house because their mother is not home. However, the Cat insists on staying and entertaining the children with a variety of unruly tricks.

The chaos continues until the fish nervously spots Mother coming down the street. The Cat quickly cleans up the house with a terrific contraption and leaves before Mother sees him. When Mother asks the children what they did while she was out, they cannot decide what to tell her. The book ends by encouraging the readers to decide what they would tell their mothers.

...the Author

Dr. Seuss was born on March 2, 1904, in Springfield, Massachusetts, as Theodore Seuss Geisel (guy-zel). Dr. Seuss graduated from Dartmouth College in 1925 and then went overseas to graduate school.

Seuss worked as an advertising artist, illustrator, cartoonist, and author, but is best known for his children's books which entertain children and adults alike. He is famous for his whimsical illustrations, zany characters, and tongue-twisting, rhythmic verse.

One of Seuss' best known works, *The Cat in the Hat,* was so successful with beginning readers that it prompted Seuss to establish Beginner Books, a company that publishes literature for young readers.

Educators began using his books to teach reading and soon the methods and philosophies of teaching reading began to change. Dr. Seuss wrote books until he was in his eighties, also using the pseudonym Theo Le Seig (created by reversing the letters in his last name). Altogether Seuss wrote 47 children's books that have sold more than two hundred million copies worldwide.

Dr. Seuss received numerous major awards. Some of these include three Caldecott Honor Awards—*McElligot's Pool* (1948), *Bartholomew and the Oobleck* (1950), and *If I Ran the Zoo* (1951); an Emmy Award—*Halloween Is Grinch Night* (1977); two Peabody Awards—*How The Grinch Stole Christmas* (1971), and *Horton Hears a Who* (1971); and in 1984, he was awarded a Pulitzer Prize for more than 50 years of dedicated work in education and entertainment.

Dr. Seuss died of cancer in La Jolla, California, in 1991, but he will always be remembered for his loveable, looney characters and his contribution to children's literature.

Suggestions for Using the Unit Activities

Use some or all of the following activities which guide the students into, through, and beyond the story with activities which promote decoding, comprehension, and appreciation of the book. To assist the teacher with planning, the suggested activities are categorized as follows:

Setting the Stage:	prereading activities and suggestions for preparing the classroom
Language Arts Activities:	activities that promote word recognition and comprehension as well as appreciation of the book
Across the Curriculum:	activities that extend the reader's understanding and appreciation of the book

Setting the Stage

1. Discuss rainy day activities and create a Rainy Day Bulletin Board. Follow the directions on page 11. A Rainy Day Fun activity student page is provided on page 12 for homework or classwork.

2. Consider using *The Cat in the Hat* to introduce your social studies unit about safety or stranger awareness.

3. Collect real hats and/or pictures of hats that can be displayed around the room to promote interest. Each day you teach the unit put on a hat (or show a picture of a hat) to signal to students that it is reading time. Encourage students to tell who would wear such a hat.

4. Set the stage and build background by discussing the following:
   - Have you ever been left alone at home? Why or why not?
   - What activities are you allowed/not allowed to do when alone?
   - Tell about a time when it took lots of courage to tell something to your parents.
   - What would you do if a stranger came to your door while you were home alone?
   - Share any experiences you have about strangers.
   - Discuss (or review from the Rainy Day Bulletin Board) rainy day activities.

5. Create folders to organize and store student work. See directions on page 13.

Language Arts Activities

1. Pocket Chart Activities: Rhyme Cards and Games

Develop a strong sight vocabulary of rhyming words to promote fluency in decoding skills. Trace cat and hat patterns from page 15 on heavy paper and write rhyming words that can be used for a variety of activities. Directions are on page 14.

Suggestions for Using the Unit Activities *(cont.)*

Language Arts Activities *(cont.)*

2. Pocket Chart Activity: Sequence Sentence Strips

To teach and practice sequencing skills, reproduce, cut out and laminate the Sequence Sentence Strips found on pages 16 and 17. Have the students put them in the correct order and display them on a pocket chart. Students may also work in groups to create a book by cutting the strips, pasting them on drawing paper, and illustrating their sentences. Staple the strips in the correct order and read them to the class.

3. Story Questions

Develop comprehension and critical thinking skills by discussing Story Questions on page 18. The questions are based on Bloom's Taxonomy and include questions at each level.

4. House Frame Poem

Have students write a poem by introducing them to a story frame form that creates a poetic-sounding summary of the story. See page 19 for directions and a sample.

5. "Who Said That?"

Have students complete page 20 to demonstrate an understanding of character traits. Remind students to use the back of the paper to complete the challenge which encourages creativity by asking students to draw the story characters and write something the character might say.

6. A Portrait of the Cat in the Hat

Have students complete page 21 to analyze the Cat's characteristics by drawing his picture and writing words to describe him.

7. Rhyme Detective

Encourage students to find rhymes directly from the story by reproducing and completing pages 22 and 23. Students will need a copy of the book to complete this activity. Working with a partner or group is recommended.

8. Picture Dictionary

Have students draw, color, cut, and assemble the Picture Dictionary on page 24 to reinforce sight vocabulary and decoding skills. After assembling the books, students can read them to partners and/or take them home to read. Students can practice alphabetical order by arranging the pages of the Picture Dictionary in ABC order.

9. Stick Puppet Drama

Let students draw, color, and cut their own characters from heavy paper and glue them to tongue depressors, or students can color, cut, and paste the patterns found on page 25. Ideas for using stick puppets are also found on page 25.

10. The Scrambler

Have students complete page 26 to practice/test decoding and comprehension skills while unscrambling the mixed-up sentences.

Suggestions for Using the Unit Activities *(cont.)*

Language Arts Activities *(cont.)*

11. Seuss-Arama Triaramas/Quadraramas

Develop summary skills by having students create three-dimensional scenes and written explanations of the beginning, middle, and end of the story. This is a good project to be completed by a group of four students. See directions and further suggestions on page 27.

12. Recorded Story

As a culminating activity, have the class work together to make a tape-recorded version of the story. Afterwards, students can listen to it at a listening center or check it out and listen to it at home. Distribute page 28 to students. Read and discuss the steps to follow for making a tape-recorded reading of the story.

13. Crossword Puzzle

Practice decoding and comprehension skills by having students complete the crossword puzzle found on page 29.

14. Context Clues

Practice or test comprehension and decoding skills by having students complete the Context Clues paragraphs on pages 30 and 31. Students having difficulty decoding should have the passage read orally to them. Let them demonstrate comprehension by choosing the word in the box that makes sense.

15. Calling All Adjectives (English/Grammar)

Let your students create original sentences and illustrations by completing a slotted sentence with adjectives. A slotted sentence leaves a word or phrase, and the answer leaves room for creativity or open-endedness. Example: The boy is a _____ (fast or slow) runner. Students can later write sentences on oaktag sentence strips to create a bulletin board. See directions on page 32.

16. Reading Wheel (Reading)

Extend reading beyond the classroom by having students read books for homework. Duplicate and hand out the Reading Wheel found on page 33. The Reading Wheel has been left blank so you can tailor the selection to fit the needs of your students. Choose other books by Dr. Seuss or related books (see the bibliography on page 48) and write the title and author on the Reading Wheel. Fill in the information at the bottom of the wheel, which reminds students how many books they are required to read and when the assignment is due. See suggestion 17 for the Book Review assignment.

17. Book Review

Students can be required to complete a Book Review page after each book they read from the Reading Wheel. This will aid in the teacher's evaluation of the students' comprehension of the book. You may staple several Book Review papers and the Reading Wheel Paper together to make a booklet. This will help to organize the assignment for you and the students. See page 34.

Suggestions for Using the Unit Activities *(cont.)*

Across the Curriculum

1. House Rules (Social Studies)

Use the story to promote an appreciation for why parents set limits and rules for their children. Have students complete page 40 for homework, writing the rules they have at their house. Discuss results in class. The rules could be written on chart paper with tally marks placed for all students with that rule in their house. Discuss the importance of rules and what the classroom, school, home, and country would be like without rules.

2. Math Code

A secret code message creates motivation for completing addition and subtraction problems on reproducible page 35.

3. Tricks (Physical Education)

Give your students an opportunity to practice and then demonstrate several physical activities that promote balance, strength, and agility, as well as fun. See page 44.

4. Weather Makes a Difference (Science)

To develop an understanding of the effects weather and seasons have on leisure activities, have students complete page 37 independently, with a partner or group, or as a whole-class discussion.

5. Hats (Social Studies)

Teach students to recognize various hats worn as either part of a costume or uniform. Complete page 39 with students. You may also want to discuss the color and function of each hat. See Setting the Stage (page 7) for other hat activities.

6. Painting Seuss-Style

Help students develop an appreciation of Seuss' drawing style by discussing the illustrations in the book and then providing students with materials to try drawing or painting like him. For a greater appreciation, study illustrations from other Seuss books as well. See page 41.

7. Other Cats in Hats (Art)

Encourage creativity by having students draw their own style of a cat wearing a hat. Use white drawing paper or duplicate page 42.

8. Cat Report (Culminating Activity)

Students will learn about a variety of cats by researching, writing, and sharing a cat report. Duplicate pages 45 and 46 to guide students. The completed report is one paragraph.

9. Seuss Award

An open-ended award can be used to motivate students or reward students during this unit. See page 47.

10. Bibliography

A list of other Dr. Seuss books as well as other related cat stories have been provided for your convenience. See page 48.

Rainy Day Bulletin Board

Materials:

- red butcher paper
- lined chart paper
- blue or white construction paper
- marking pens
- crayons

Engage prior knowledge and oral language skills by having students discuss rainy day activities and then create a bulletin board displaying their ideas.

Directions:

1. Prepare a red house background (see sample bulletin board below). Measure your chart paper and then add 4" (10.16 cm) to the dimensions. Use the new dimensions to create a red rectangular house. Add a red roof, chimney, and steps.

2. Use your own lettering to create a Rainy Day Fun caption.

3. Cut a large blue (or white) raindrop for each student in your class, or make a pattern and let students cut their own.

4. Discuss rainy day activities. The Rainy Day Fun student page can be completed during this lesson or for homework before or after the lesson. (See page 12.)

5. Ask all of the students to tell you something they like to do on a rainy day. Write their responses on the chart in pen. (Short phrases or one-word answers work best so they can be easily read.)

6. Students trace words with markers and decorate the raindrops with crayons.

7. Staple lined paper on the house, completing the bulletin board.

Name _____

Rainy Day Fun

The children in *The Cat in the Hat* did not know what to do on such a rainy day. Think of 10 things you can do on a rainy day and write them in the raindrops. Then write some sentences about your favorite rainy day in the space below.

My Favorite Rainy Day Fun

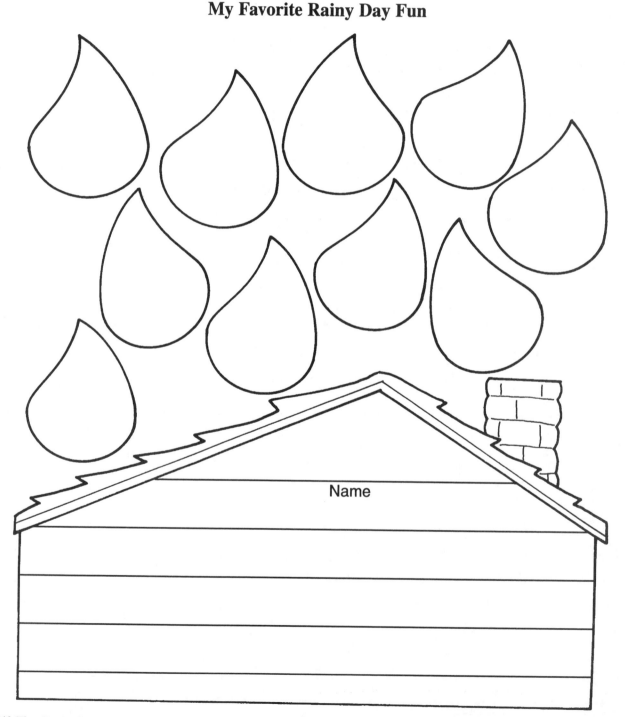

Name

Reading Folders

These folders will help organize and store students' work.

Materials:

- construction paper (12"x18" / 30 cm x 46 cm)
- crayons
- pencils

Directions:

Hand each student a piece of construction paper.   Fold it in half; write the title of the book and author's name on the front. Encourage students to decorate their folders with pictures of the Cat.

Staple the Sight Words list on the inside cover of the folder. This list can be used as a diagnosis of the student's sight vocabulary or can be sent home for students to practice for homework.

Sight Words

shine	nothing	saw	our	take
play	house	said	white	mother
cold	cat	why	when	thing
day	could	have	these	should
there	was	good	what	wall
two	like	know	little	head
out	looked	your	this	something

Pocket Chart Rhyme Cards and Games

These activities will promote rhyming skills and encourage students to see that rhyming words can have dissimilar spellings. Students will also build fluency in decoding skills.

The following directions will make one set of cards to be used by the entire class. Use any color of heavy paper and laminate it, if possible.

Directions:

1. Reproduce the cat and hat patterns found on the next page. Trace and cut 24 hats and 24 cats from the heavy paper.

2. Print one word on each card to make flashcards.

3. Complete some or all of the following rhyme card activities.

✳	Cat Word Cards		✳	✳	Hat Word Cards		✳
play	cat	man	gown	day	that	fan	down
two	sunny	said	fear	do	funny	head	hear
ball	say	pot	you	all	away	not	to
sit	fish	so	yes	bit	dish	know	mess
bump	now	fox	go	jump	how	box	no
mat	cake	hook	hall	hat	rake	look	wall

- Matching Game: Use enough sets of rhyming cards so that each student has one card. Shuffle the cards and pass one to each student. When you say "Rhyme Time," have students stand up, walk around the room and find someone who has a card that rhymes. They should then sit together and wait for the rest of the class to finish. Try timing the class to create motivation.

- Keep the words in a box or basket (or even a hat) and let students find rhymes and display them on the wall chart.

- Sort the cards into two sets: cat cards and hat cards. Keep the hat cards and pass each student one or more cat cards. The leader of the game (teacher or student) will take a hat card from the top of the pile and say "I'm looking for a cat who could wear this hat." Then the leader calls out the word on the hat card. The student with the rhyming cat card should stand, say the word on his/her card and then receive the hat card and sit down. Time the class to see how quickly they can complete the task.

Pocket Chart Rhyme Card Patterns

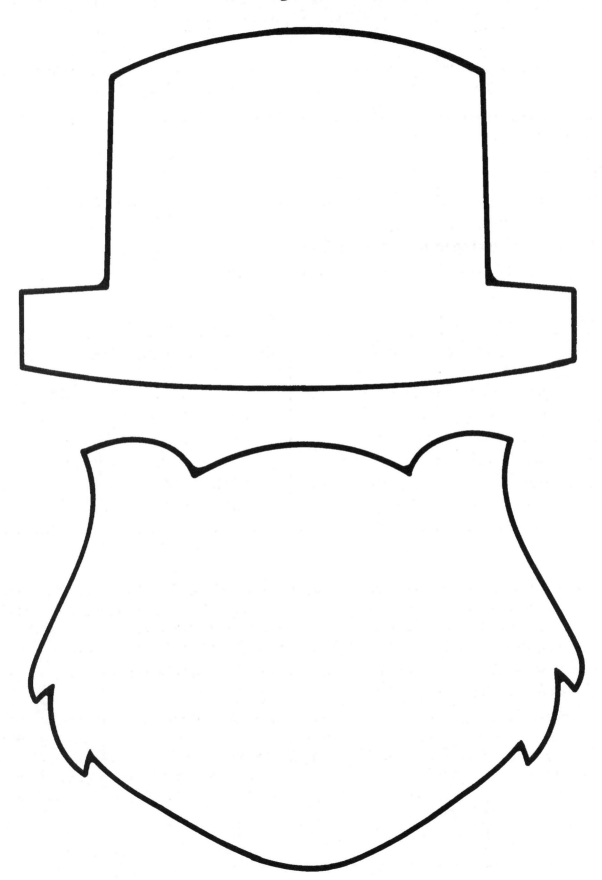

Pocket Chart Sequence Sentence Strips

(See page 8, suggestion two.)

It is raining, so Sally and her brother have nothing to do.

The Cat in the Hat comes to the house.

The Cat wants to do tricks, but the fish tells him to go away.

The Cat does not listen to the fish and starts to do his tricks and messes up the house.

Pocket Chart Sequence Sentence Strips *(cont.)*

Mother can be seen coming down the street.
The Cat cleans the house and leaves.
Mother comes in the house and asks the children to tell her about their day.
The children do not know whether or not to tell their mother about the Cat.

Story Questions

The following questions are based on Bloom's Taxonomy. Discuss these questions after reading the story.

I. Knowledge (ability to recall learned information)

    A. Students tell what kind of day it was.

    B. Who comes to visit the children?

    C. Why does the Fish think the Cat should leave?

    D. Name three things the Cat did while in the house.

    E. How did the house get cleaned up?

II. Comprehension (basic understanding of information)

    A. Do you think the story takes place now or long ago?

    B. Do you think the Cat wanted to cause trouble?

    C. Why do you suppose the children allowed the Cat to stay?

    D. What finally made the Cat leave?

III. Application (ability to do something new with information)

    A. How do you think the children felt when they saw their mother coming down the street?

    B. Predict what would have happened if the Cat had not cleaned up the mess.

    C. What do you suppose the children will do and say if a stranger comes to their door again?

    D. What do you think Mother would have done if she had walked in while the Cat was doing his tricks?

    E. Have you ever done something you were not supposed to do? Did you tell anyone about it?

IV. Analysis (ability to examine the parts of a whole)

    A. Why do you think the cat came to visit?

    B. Why do you think the children let the cat in?

    C. Why do you think the cat cleaned up his mess?

    D. Why do you think the children had a hard time telling their mother about their day?

    E. Why do you think it took so long before the children told the cat to go away?

V. Synthesis (ability to bring together information to make something new)

    A. Do you think the Cat's tricks were fun?

    B. Tell some other things the cat could have done with the children.

    C. Tell the good and bad characteristics of the Cat.

    D. Tell what you would have done to get rid of the Cat.

    E. Would the story have been different if the visitor had been an elephant instead of a cat?

VI. Evaluation (ability to form and defend an opinion)

    A. Do you think the children learned a lesson? Why?

    B. Do you like the Cat? Tell why.

    C. Would you want the Cat to come to your house? Why?

    D. Would you recommend this story to a friend? Why?

House Frame Poem

Students can summarize the story by writing this poetic-sounding framed story.

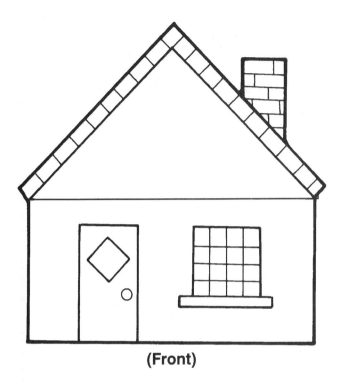

(Front)

Materials:

- red construction paper (9" x 12" / 23 cm x 30 cm)
- white construction paper (4½" x 6" / 11.4 cm x 15 cm)
- glue
- scissors
- pencil
- black felt tip pen

Directions:

1. On the red paper, have students draw a house. (Encourage them to draw it as large as possible.)
2. Cut it out and decorate the roof and window with the white paper.
3. Write the story frame on the back of the house. Let the triangular roof shape be a guideline for the shape of the writing. See example below.

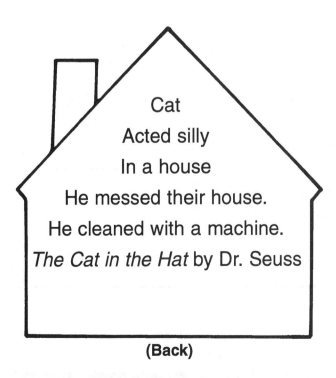

Cat
Acted silly
In a house
He messed their house.
He cleaned with a machine.
The Cat in the Hat by Dr. Seuss

(Back)

Line 1 - (1 word) State the character's name.

Line 2 - (2 words) Describe the character.

Line 3 - (3 words) Tell the setting.

Line 4 - (4 words) State the problem.

Line 5 - (5 words) State the solution.

Line 6 - Give the title and author of the story.

Name _____

"Who Said That?"

Read each quotation. Tell whether the Boy, the Fish, or the Cat is speaking. Write your answer.

1. "Look at me! Look at me! Look at me now!"

    _____

2. "Put me down!"

    _____

3. "If Mother could see this, Oh, what would she say?"

    _____

4. "Have no fear, little fish..."

    _____

5. "I know it is wet and the sun is not sunny."

    _____

6. "So all we could do was to Sit! Sit! Sit! Sit!"

    _____

✦Challenge:

On the back of this page, write something each character might say and draw the character next to the quotation.

Name _____

A Portrait of The Cat in the Hat

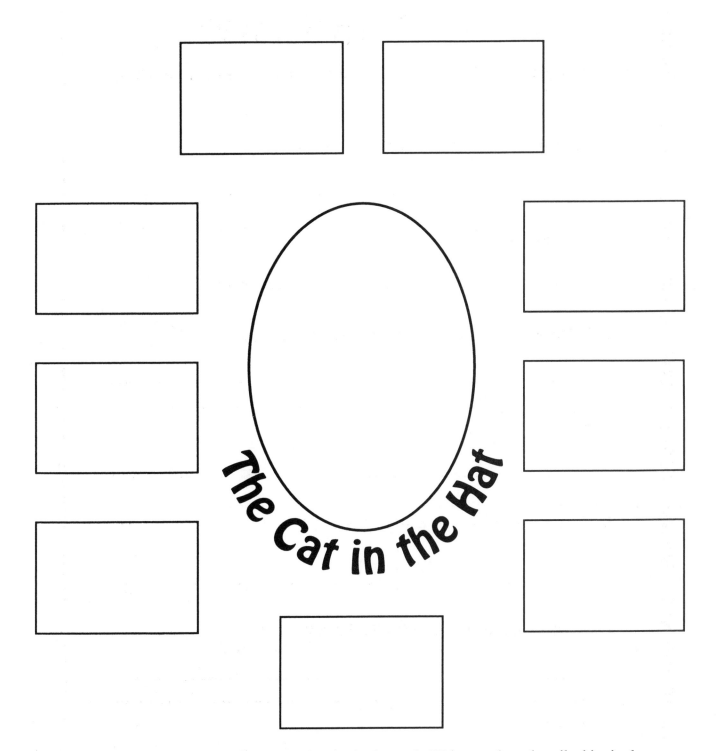

Directions: Draw the cat from *The Cat in the Hat* in the oval. Write words to describe him in the boxes.

Name _____

Rhyme Detective

The star (☆) below will tell you where in your book to look for a word that rhymes with each of the following. Write the rhyming words in the boxes below.

1. Page 1   **play**

2. Page 5   **bump**

3. Page 7   **sunny**

4. Page 12   **wish**

5. Page 21   **fall**

Name_____

Rhyme Detective *(cont.)*

How many more rhyming words can you find in your book? Write them in the boxes.

⑥	★ Page 28	**box**	
⑦	★ Page 29	**hook**	
⑧	★ Page 35	**not**	
⑨	★ Page 40	**hall**	
⑩	★ Page 42	**gown**	

Picture Dictionary

Directions:

1. Trace each word.
2. Illustrate each word.
3. Cut on solid black lines.

4. Make a cover from construction paper.
5. Staple.
6. Read.

cat	hat
ball	book
dish	cake
rake	ship
cup	fish

Stick Puppet Patterns and Activity Ideas

Let students work in groups to dramatize the story for the class. Let students create new stories and situations, using the puppets. The teacher can tell something that one of the characters did in the story, and the students can hold up the puppet he/she was referring to. (Example: "Which character visited the house?" The students hold up the Cat puppet.)

Cat

Thing One

Thing Two

Sally

Brother

Fish

Name _____

The Scrambler

Directions: Unscramble each set of words to make a complete sentence. Write the sentence on the line.

Hint: Start each sentence with the word that is capitalized.

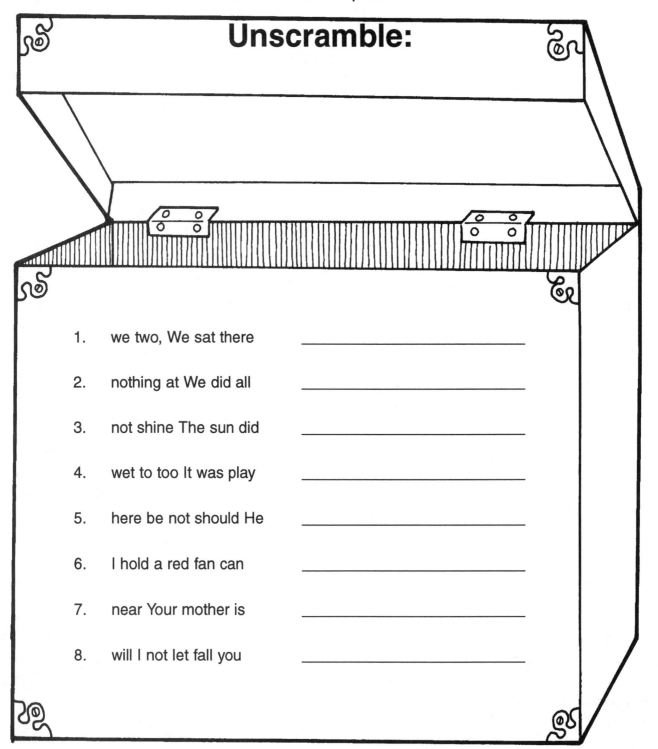

Unscramble:

1.　we two, We sat there　　_____

2.　nothing at We did all　　_____

3.　not shine The sun did　　_____

4.　wet to too It was play　　_____

5.　here be not should He　　_____

6.　I hold a red fan can　　_____

7.　near Your mother is　　_____

8.　will I not let fall you　　_____

Seuss-Arama Triarama

A triarama is a three-dimensional art and writing project that lets students creatively reflect upon what they have learned.

Students can glue four triaramas together to create a quadrarama.

Materials:

- construction paper (9"/ 23 cm square)
- construction paper scraps
- scissors
- glue
- crayon, markers, pencils
- index card (cut lengthwise into thirds)

Directions:

1. Fold on each diagonal.

2. Open and cut from one point to center.

3. Draw a background scene on half of the square, as shown.

4. Overlap the two bottom triangles and glue.

5. Glue scraps of construction paper to the stand-up parts to decorate the triarama.

6. Write about the story on the index card and glue it to the front of the triarama base.

Suggestion: Make quadraramas and include a *title* and *author*, a *beginning*, a *conflict*, and a *solution*.

Recorded Story

Make a tape-recorded reading of the story. Afterwards, use headphones and listen to the story during your free time.

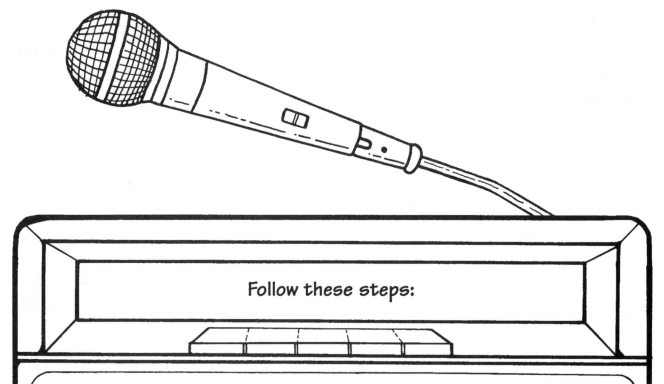

Follow these steps:

1. Choose a part of the story to read. (Your teacher may assign you a part.)

2. With a partner, practice reading with expression.

3. Sit in the order in which you will be reading your part.

4. Listen and watch as your teacher explains how to use the recorder and microphone to record your parts.

5. One at a time, you and the other readers will come up to the tape recorder and slowly read the parts you have been practicing.

6. When you have finished recording, rewind the tape. Listen to and enjoy your tape-recorded reading of the story.

Name _____

Crossword Puzzle

Across

1. Who left the house for the day?

4. Did the Fish like the Cat in their house?

6. The day was not _____ because the sun was not out.

Down

1. The Cat made a _____ in the house.

2. Another name for "kids"

3. Why it was wet outside

5. Thing _____ and Thing Two

Name _____

Context Clues

Read the entire story. Look at the list of words below. Reread the story and fill in the blanks with a word that makes sense. Use each word once.

wet	**out**	**tricks**	**house**
bump	**girl**	**Fish**	**Cat**

Part One

Once there was a boy and a _____ .

One day their mother went _____ . The

children felt sad because it was raining and it was too

_____ to play. Then something went

_____ at their door.

It was the _____ . The Cat came in

and played some _____ . He messed up

their _____ . The

_____ told him to go away, but he

did not.

Name _____

Context Clues *(cont.)*

Read the entire story. Go back and fill in the blanks with a word that makes sense. Use each word once.

say   **cleaned**   **Mother**

machine   **day**   **tricks**

Part Two

The Cat played more _____ . But then

they saw _____ coming down

the street.

The Cat left and came back with a big

_____ .

He _____ the house and put

everything away.

When Mother came home, she wanted to know what

the children had done all _____ .

What do you think they should _____?

Name _____

Calling All Adjectives

Adjective: An adjective is a word that describes a noun.

Directions: Brainstorm adjectives to fit in the blanks. Then choose your two favorite words and write them in the sentence. Draw a picture of your sentence in the box below.

Examples:	fat	red
	brave	tall

_____   _____

_____   _____

_____   _____

_____   _____

_____   _____

_____   _____

A _____ cat in a _____ hat ran away.
    (fat)   (red)

Picture Sentence Box

Reading Wheel

Each time you read a book, fill in the wheel segment and color it. You are now ready to complete a book review of your book(s). Your teacher will give you further instructions on the number of books to be read, the number of book reviews to be completed, and their due dates.

Name_____

Number of books to be read _____

Number of book reviews to be completed _____

Due date _____

Name _____

Book Review

Read a book and then fill in the information below.

Title _____

Author _____

Characters _____

_____

Setting _____

_____

The story was about _____

_____

_____

_____.

My favorite part was _____

_____

_____

_____.

I would/would not recommend this book to a friend because
(*circle one*)

_____

_____

_____.

Name_____

Math Code

After reading *The Cat in the Hat*, use the Math Code to answer the riddle by solving the equations below. Then match the number and write each letter in its own answer box.

Who do you find in a big red box?

0	9	7	6	10	2	5	8	3	4
N	H	O	E	T	D	I	G	A	W

9	4	3	5	4		8	6	9
+1	+5	+2	−5	+4		−1	−6	−3

2	0	4		8	8	4	9	9		2	9	6
+1	+0	−2		+2	+1	+1	−9	−1		+8	−5	+1

Kite Math

A Kite Graph

Materials

- white construction paper for kite (3"/ 8 cm square)
- pencils
- crayons
- any color yarn
- glue

Directions:

After reading *The Cat in the Hat* students answer the question: Have you ever flown a kite? Have students graph their "Yes" or "No" responses. Have students cut out kite shapes from white construction paper. Ask each student to write his or her name in a shape, decorate it, and attach a yarn tail to one corner. Use the students' kites to create a graph that can be used as a hands-on bulletin board. Children staple their kites directly onto the bulletin board as shown, or they may be attached to chart paper with glue.

Toothpick Kite Math

Materials:

- light blue construction paper (9" / 23 cm square)
- flat toothpicks
- pencils

Directions:

Using flat toothpicks, have students create number sentences with the sum of 7. Discuss possible number sentences. Possibilities could include: 5+2=7, 2+5=7, 7+0=7, 6+1=7, 1+6=7, 4+3=7. Brainstorm as a whole class and list students' responses.

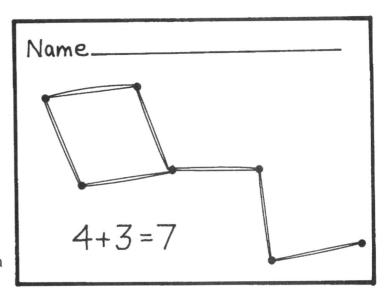

Students glue toothpicks (seven) on paper in a number sentence in which the sum is seven. For example, students may choose to glue four toothpicks on their paper, followed by three more in the shape of a tail. The students complete this activity by writing out the number sentence they created. (See illustration.)

Weather Makes a Difference

In the boxes below, write about or draw a picture of what you like to do on each kind of day.

❖ **Challenge:** On the back of this page, write a story about your favorite sunny, rainy, snowy, or windy day activity.

Wind

Materials:

- kite
- white butcher paper (enough to record students' responses)
- pencils
- open field or area to demonstrate kite flying with your class

Directions:

Discuss why a kite flies (what it needs). Ask students if they know what makes a kite fly. Does shape have anything to do with it? What about the wind? Discuss aerodynamics (streamlined for flying). What does the tail do? Why is it needed (balance)? Before leading a demonstration of kite flying, predict and record (graph) what the class thinks will happen to the kite. Will the kite have too much wind, just the right amount, or not enough? List and record students' names under the appropriate response.

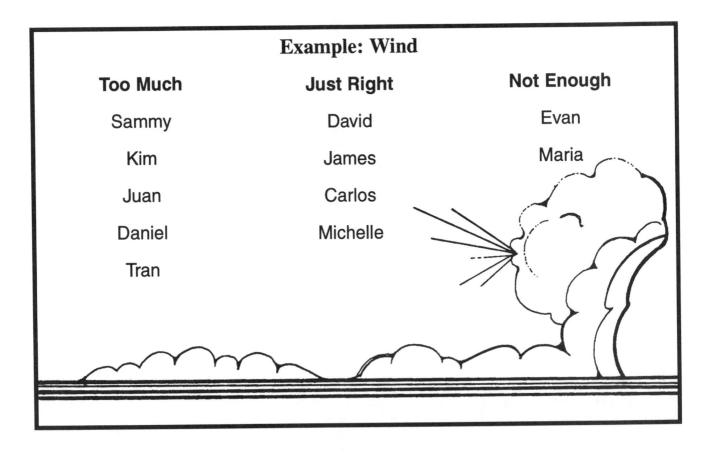

Example: Wind

Too Much	Just Right	Not Enough
Sammy	David	Evan
Kim	James	Maria
Juan	Carlos	
Daniel	Michelle	
Tran		

Take the class outdoors to an open field so they may fly the kite. Test wind prediction and discuss actual results. Ask students the following question: Did your predictions match your results? Compare the prediction graph to the students' responses (actual results) after flying the kite.

Name _____

Hats

The Cat wore a hat that we would recognize anywhere. Here are some other hats that tell us something about the people wearing them. How many can you recognize? Use the Word Bank below to label the hats on this page.

Word Bank

sailor	chef	police officer
cowboy/cowgirl	nurse	clown
baseball player	firefighter	magician

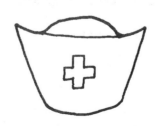

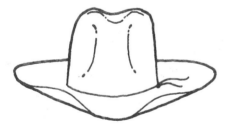

_____   _____   _____

House Rules

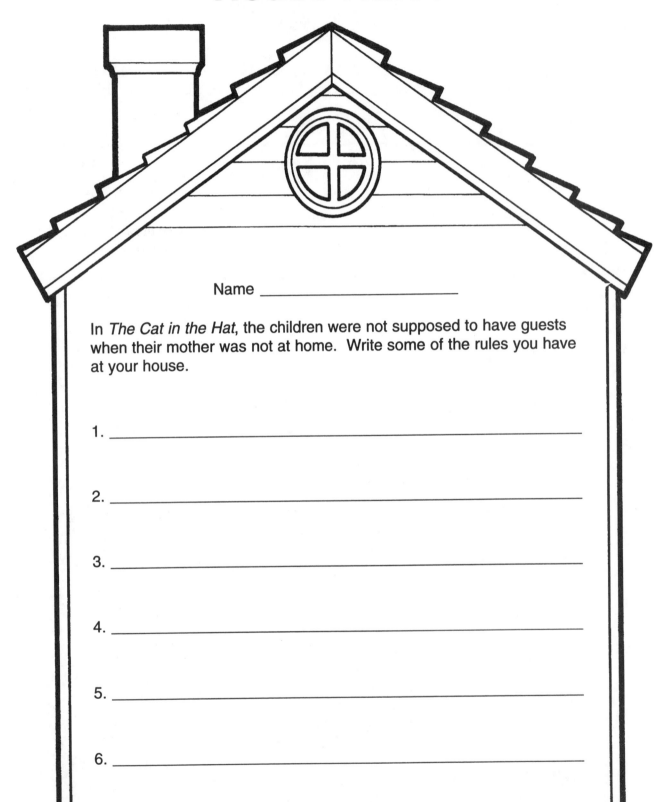

Name _____

In *The Cat in the Hat*, the children were not supposed to have guests when their mother was not at home. Write some of the rules you have at your house.

1. _____

2. _____

3. _____

4. _____

5. _____

6. _____

7. _____

Painting Seuss-Style

Materials:

- heavy white paper (15" x 20" / 38 cm x 51 cm)
- tempera paint (red, blue, white, black)
- tagboard sentence strips
- marking pens/brushes
- clear plastic book report covers (optional)

Observe Illustrations:

- Discuss Dr. Seuss's style of illustration. Have students look at illustrations and notice the colors (red, blue, white, and black), the shape of the lines (all curved), the way he drew characters (especially eyes and mouths), and the texture of the pictures (everything is painted in a smooth, flat, solid tone).

Painting Directions:

- Have students choose a picture from the story. To achieve the style, the students need to look at the picture in the book while they draw and paint. (Cover the page with the plastic book report cover to keep it clean.)

- Draw with pencil and then paint. Be sure students outline their paintings with black (paint or markers) to achieve the style.

Writing Captions:

- Students can write captions describing their paintings on sentence strips.

- Hang the paintings. Collect the sentence strips. To develop listening skills, have each student read his caption and let the rest of the class guess which painting is being described. Then hang the captions.

Other Cats in Hats

Using his imagination, Dr. Seuss drew the Cat in *The Cat in the Hat*. Use your imagination to create your own cat in the hat. Make any kind of cat and any kind of hat. Use your own colors, too.

42

Kites

The Things fly kites in *The Cat in the Hat*. Try making some kites.

Windy Kites

Materials:

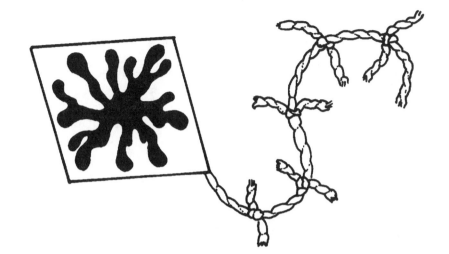

- white construction paper
  (6" / 15 cm square)
- red tempera paint
- red yarn
- straw(s)
- glue
- newsprint or newspaper

Directions:

Discuss and review why a kite flies. What does it need? Place newsprint or newspaper on the work area or table. Place the kite paper on top of the newsprint or newspaper. Squeeze a drop of paint (red) on the kite paper. Gently blow into the straw to spread the paint. Glue on a red yarn tail. Display finished kites.

Soaring Kites

Materials:

- white butcher paper
  (12" / 30 cm square)
- any color yarn
- black crayon(s)
- watercolor paints
- stapler
- pencils (optional)

Directions:

Students will need two kite papers each. They will draw a self portrait on each paper with their black crayons(s). They will then use the watercolors to paint pictures of themselves. Staple both kite papers together, making sure that on each side the portrait is facing out so it is looking at you. (**Hint:** Only staple halfway up the kite in order to leave enough room to stuff or fill the kite.) Use paper to stuff or fill the kite. Staple it closed. Place a hole near the top with a hole-puncher in order to hang these three-dimensional kites. Attach the yarn tail, as shown in the illustration.

Name _____

Tricks

The Cat in *The Cat in the Hat* liked playing tricks and doing stunts. How many of these stunts can you do? Try them and check (✔) the ones you can do.

☐ 1. Stand on one foot.

☐ 2. Snap your fingers.

☐ 3. Balance a book on your head.

☐ 4. Walk with a book balanced on your head.

☐ 5. Spin a ball on one finger.

☐ 6. Do three push-ups.

☐ 7. Balance a stack of pennies on the back of your hand.

The following are outside tricks. Please get help from your teacher.

☐ 8. Stand on your head.

☐ 9. Do a cartwheel.

☐ 10. Do a somersault.

Cat Report

Choose one of the cats from the list in the box. Follow the steps to write a report.

1. Choose a cat. Write the name of the cat here:

    _____

2. Choose a book about the cat. Write the name of the book and the author here:

    _____

    _____

3. Read the book (or have an adult read it to you).

4. Answer the questions on page 46.

5. Use your answers to write a paragraph about the cat.

6. Draw and color a picture of the cat.

7. Make a report cover.

8. Staple the report cover, the paragraph, and the drawing together.

CATS
Siamese Cat
Persian Cat
Puma
Jaguar
Cheetah
Lion
Panther
Tiger
Bobcat
Lynx
Ocelot

Cat Report *(cont.)*

Use the following questions to write a paragraph about your cat. Also, include your illustration.

What cat did you choose? _____

_____

Describe how it looks:

Color _____

Size _____

Special Markings_____

Other _____

Cat Illustration

_____

_____

Where does it live? _____

_____

_____

What does it eat? _____

_____

_____

List any other interesting facts: _____

_____

_____

Seuss-Award

Presented to _____

For _____

Date _____

Signed _____

Bibliography

Self-Illustrated Writings Under the Pseudonym Dr. Seuss

And To Think I Saw It On Mulberry Street, Vanguard, 1937.

The 500 Hats of Bartholomew Cubbins, Vanguard, 1938.

The Seven Lady Godivas, Random House, 1939, reprinted, 1987.

The King's Stilts, Random House, 1940.

Mc Elligot's Pool, Random House, 1947.

Thidwick, the Big-Hearted Moose, Random House, 1948.

Bartholomew and the Oobleck, Random House, 1949.

If I Ran the Zoo, Random House, 1950.

Scrambled Eggs Super! Random House, 1953.

The Sneetches and Other Stories, Random House, 1954.

On Beyond Zebra, Random House, 1955.

If I Ran The Circus, Random House, 1956.

Signs of Civilization! (booklet), La Jolla Town Council, 1956.

The Cat In The Hat, Random House, 1957, French/English edition published as *La Chat au Chapeau,* Random House, 1967, Spanish/English edition published as *El Gato ensombrerado,* Random House, 1967.

How the Grinch Stole Christmas (also see below), Random House, 1957.

The Cat In The Hat Comes Back!, Beginner Books, 1958.

Yertle the Turtle and Other Stories, Random House, 1958.

Happy Birthday to You!, Random House, 1959.

One Fish, Two Fish, Red Fish, Blue Fish, Random House, 1960.

Green Eggs and Ham, Beginner Books, 1960.

Dr. Seuss' Sleep Book, Random House, 1962.

Hop on Pop, Beginner Books, 1963.

Dr. Seuss' ABC, Beginner Books, 1963.

(With Phillip D. Eastman) *The Cat In The Hat Dictionary,* Beginner Books, 1964.

Horton Hears a Who! (also see below) Random House, 1954.

The Cat In The Hat Songbook, Random House, 1967.

The Dr. Seuss Storybook (Includes *Scrambled Eggs Super!*), Collins, 1974.

Cats

dePaola, Tomie. *Kids' Cat Book.* Holiday House, 1979.

DeRegniers, Beatrice. *So Many Cats.* Houghton, 1985.

Eisler, Colin. *Cats Know Best.* Dial Books, 1988.

Geraghty, Paul. *Slobcat.* Macmillan, 1991.

Goodall, John. *The Surprise Picnic.* Macmillan, 1977.

Griffith, Helen V. *Alex and the Cat.* Greenwillow, 1982.

Hawkins, Colin. *Pat the Cat.* Putnam, 1986.

Hersom, Kathleen and Donald Hersom. *The Copycat.* Macmillan, 1991.

Hogrogian, Nonny. *The Cat Who Loved to Sing.* Knopf, 1988.

James, Betsy. *He Wakes Me.* Orchard, 1991.

Keats, Ezra. *Hi Cat!* Macmillan, 1988.

Keats, Ezra. *Kitten for a Day.* Macmillan, 1984.

Kulling, Monica. *I Hate You, Marmalade!* Viking, 1992.

Lindstrom, Eva. *Cat Hat.* Kane\Miller Book Publisher, 1989.

Marshall, Val. *Cat's Whiskers.* SRA, 1994.

McPhail, David. *Great Cat.* Dutton, 1986.

Reiser, Lynn. *Bedtime Cat.* Greenwillow, 1991.

Wiseman, Bernard. *Cats! Cats! Cats!* Parents, 1984.

Wolff, Ashley. *Only the Cat Saw.* Puffin, 1988.

Hats

Blos, Joan W. *Martin's Hats.* Morrow, 1984.

Clark, Emma. *Catch That Hat.* Little, 1990.

Geringer, Laura. *A Three Hat Day.* Harper, 1985.

Howard, Elizabeth. *Aunt Flossie's Hats.* Houghton, 1991.

Lindbergh, Anne. *Next Time, Take Care.* Harcourt, 1988.

Miller, Margaret. *Whose Hat?* Greenwillow, 1988.

Morris, Ann. *Hats, Hats, Hats.* Morrow, 1989.

Roy, Ron. *Whose Hat Is That?* Clarion, 1990.

Smith, William. *Ho for Hat!* Little, 1989.

Van Laan, Nancy. *This Is the Hat: A Story in Rhyme.* Little, 1992.

Wildsmith, Brian. *What Did I Find?* Harcourt, 1993.

48